UPDATED

THE
MONEY MAP

FINALLY... YOUR SIMPLE ONE PAGE PLAN FOR RETIREMENT AND INVESTMENT SUCCESS

D0822542

Maggie Knoedler Rueda
Journey of Yoga

UPDATED

THE
MONEY MAP

FINALLY... YOUR SIMPLE ONE PAGE PLAN
FOR RETIREMENT AND INVESTMENT SUCCESS

JOEL M. JOHNSON, CFP

Copyright © 2011. 2014 by Joel M. Johnson

Printed in the United States of America.

ISBN: 978-1-59571-645-3

Designed and published by

Word Association Publishers
205 Fifth Avenue
Tarentum, Pennsylvania 15084

www.wordassociation.com
1.800.827.7903

TABLE OF CONTENTS

REGULATORY ISSUES
NOTE TO READERS

This publication contains the opinions and ideas of its author. The strategies outlined in this book may not be suitable for every individual and are not guaranteed or warranted to produce any particular results. Presentation of performance data herein does not imply that similar results will be achieved in the future. Any such data is provided merely for illustrative and discussion purposes; rather than focusing on the time periods used or the results derived, the reader should focus instead on the underlying principles.

This book is sold with the understanding that neither publisher nor author, through his book, is engaged in rendering legal, tax, investment, insurance, financial, accounting, or other professional advice or services. If the reader requires such advice or services, a competent professional should be consulted. Relevant laws vary from state to state.

No warranty is made with respect to the accuracy or the completeness of the information contained herein, and both the author and the publisher specifically disclaim any responsibility for any liability, loss, or risk, personal or otherwise, that is incurred as a consequence, directly or indirectly, of the use and application of any of the contents of this book.

Last, this book is written under the Right of the 1st amendment to the Constitution of the United States.

INTRODUCTION TO THE MONEY MAP

Over the past 16 years I have personally met with thousands of people—families and individuals, rich and poor, young and old, those who are brilliant and others of average intelligence. I have helped many of these people, but unfortunately some of them decided not to follow the advice they were given. In essence, they were unwilling to be helped. When that happened, some of those folks paid a dear, dear price. I can think of countless individuals who came back to my firm a year after listening to our recommendations but not following them; they had hundreds of thousands, maybe even millions of dollars less than they had had earlier. Sometimes these losses were due to bad advice from another broker, sometimes it was because of fear, and sometimes simply because they found it hard to make changes.

There are a number of reasons why individuals and families don't do the right thing when it comes to their money. We're going to explore that in the Money Map, but more important, we're going to explore ways that you can get your financial house in order in a very simple way.

In this book I will share some of the secrets that I have learned over my 26 years in the investment and retirement planning business. I will also share with you some of the dirty little secrets of Wall Street, some of the things that go on behind the scenes that can hurt your financial security.

I look forward to your exploring these strategies that we put together in this book and bettering your financial future for the benefit of yourself and your family.

A little bit about myself: I, along with my business partners have built a firm that now employs 18 people. Together we serve hundreds of clients in the greater northeastern part of our United States. We do investment planning and insurance planning. We help clients to reduce taxes and to grow wealth. Our primary focus is on helping retirees to protect their nest eggs, to grow their nest eggs, and maybe even more important than that, to keep their nest eggs safe from the people who are trying to take their money. Taxes, lawyers, and even our local and state governments are all in line to take our money. Sometimes it's that son or daughter-in-law who is in line to take our money. How do we protect our money? How do we grow our money? How can we ensure that our retirement reflects our goals and values in life and is not filled with the worry that many Americans have of running out of money before they die?

HEY, WHERE ARE YOU GOING?
GOALS: CHOOSING A DESTINATION

Begin with the end in mind—Steven Covey

Here's a great exercise I have my clients do in the planning process that is very effective and helps visually clarify a destination. I will tell them, "Pretend there were no restrictions or rules, and forget everything you think you know about your financial situation. If you could wave a magic wand and solve your biggest financial concern right now, what would that problem be? Go ahead—on a separate piece of paper write down that problem. Next, write down all the feelings you would have if this one issue was fixed. After that, close your eyes and visualize exactly what the outcome would look like. How would it change your life? How would it change your relationships? Again, how would you feel?"

The most important question I then ask is, "Do you want me to help you fix this problem?"

As an advisor, I can help only if people want me to help, but it's very important that they choose their goals and tell me what their financial concerns are. The problem in this business of giving financial advice is that too many financial advisors go to client meetings with their own agenda. They want to sell an annuity, a mutual fund, or some horrible life insurance policy. They want to sell the latest and greatest scheme that their Wall Street brokerage firm has come up with to make money. Again, it's not about the client, is it? No.

In our practice it *is* about the client, and we simply ask people, "What are your concerns?" And then we help them decide if they are prepared to take action to address those concerns. Can they be fixed? Then we simply ask the client, "Would you like me to help you fix this?" And that is the exact wording I use. "Would you like me to help you fix this?"

So being financially successful takes knowing your destination and understanding why it is important for you to get there. Not just the logical reasons or benefits, but the emotional reasons. One of the most important words I used in this chapter so far is *feelings*. Emotions, not logic, dictate our human behavior. A concern is emotional. A financial concern is emotional. A fear is emotional. The first item on your Money Map should be your biggest concern. When you have identified where you are going, a good advisor can help you get there.

Once you have expressed a goal, it is time to figure out how you can get there. Most financial goals take money. To reach these goals, changes need to be made. Many of the changes we help our clients make involve changing investment strategies. We use different investment tools than most firms out there, tools that can deliver more-predictable returns. It is amazing how many times I have a client tell me, "Well, Fidelity or Merrill Lynch told me all I can depend on is a 4% rate of return." Well folks, you shouldn't be paying somebody to get a 4% rate of return; for heaven's sakes you can get that on your own. Let's be realistic here. The job of a financial advisor is to get a better rate of return than you can get on your own, to coach you into establishing realistic goals, and to help you when the going gets tough.

Sometimes it means going in a direction that is counterintuitive, such as delaying saving for retirement in order to pay down debt. Another counterintuitive decision that I have recommended before is the following: if you have to choose between saving for your retirement and saving for your kids' education, then save for retirement. Look at it this way: your kids can take out student loans or work while in college or both. Believe me, they will be okay, and maybe even better off because of it. However, if you don't save for your retirement, you'll be living with your well-educated kids. Is that what you want? Tough choices have to be made. That is why it is so important to *feel* the benefits of the goal. Only then will you be able to make those tough choices and stick with them.

Remember to begin with the end in mind: literally write it down. Be crystal clear. We like our clients to write it down on their Money Maps in their own handwriting, and then our mission is to help them reach their goal. Get a coach, a financial advisor who can help you reach your goal. (Later on in this book I will tell you how to choose a financial advisor.)

One last item to keep in mind: just as successful athletes focus on one game or match at a time, successful investors focus on one issue at a time. They fix it, and then they move on to the next one.

TAKING ADVICE FROM BIASED SOURCES

Many people act on advice from parties they don't even know. Sometimes the advice comes from financial magazines or from somebody on TV, maybe even a book like this one. We need to be very careful of this. As a general rule, do not act on advice from anyone who does not know your individual situation—everyone's finances are unique. What might be great advice for one person might be terrible advice for another. In fact, it may be advice that financially ruins the other person. Think of a doctor's prescription that could save one person's life yet kill another.

The other critical fact we have to understand is that at times advice comes from biased sources, from individuals who have a direct financial interest in your being steered a certain way. It is so important if you're using a financial advisor, which I recommend that you do, that you find somebody you can trust, someone who shares your values.

Let's talk about the relationship with your doctor for a minute. Do you trust your doctor? I feel very good about mine, who has been my doctor for at least 18 years. He is about seven miles away from my house, and he knows my situation, I feel very comfortable with him. He's caring. He always returns phone calls the same day; I can't think of a time that he has not. So I appreciate my doctor.

But let me ask you if your doctor makes more money if he performs an operation on you or if he simply gives you exercises to do to solve, let's say, a knee injury. An orthopedic surgeon can operate on you and make a lot of money—Oh, yeah. Orthopedic surgeons make a lot. But such a surgeon may also recommend just some exercise, maybe swimming or stretching exercises that will solve the problem. You have to trust that if he recommends knee surgery, it is indeed in your best interest—he could be biased and trying just to make extra money.

Now let's talk about some of the biases in the financial services business. First of all, let's consider financial magazines; you can typically find anywhere from five to fifteen financial publications just at your grocery store. *Money Magazine, Forbes, Fortune, Worth,* and various other publications will offer you financial advice. But how do these magazines really make money? Advertising revenues, for the most part; the subscription price really just covers the distribution. Next time you're in a grocery store, pick up one of those magazines and look at the back cover, and then the inside front cover, and then the inside back cover, the most expensive spots to advertise. Then look inside at the full-page ads. The biggest advertisers in these magazines are for the most part mutual fund firms and Wall Street firms. It might say *Wells Fargo Bank,* it might say *Bank of America,* but what they are really selling is their investment services business.

These magazines come out with a top-10 list every year. You know what I mean: *Money Magazine* will list this year's top 10 mutual funds or the worst-performing funds. Let's say a mutual fund company such as Franklin Templeton buys the back covers of *Money Magazine* throughout the year. Do you know how much money that costs? It's a substantial commitment for Franklin Templeton, probably in the multimillions of dollars. Do you think that when *Money Magazine* puts together its worst-funds list in a certain year it is going to be a little biased to make sure that Franklin Templeton doesn't get on that list? Maybe. I don't know. I'm not saying the people at *Money Magazine* are good or bad; I'm just trying to point out a potential bias in the market place.

Let's talk about another bias. Do Wall Street firms make more money selling you risky investments or selling you safe investments? When I say safe, I mean investments that either cannot go down or offer the investor an extremely low probability of losing value—something with some type of a guarantee, preferably a government guarantee. So I ask the question again, do Wall Street firms make more money off of you when your money is safe or at risk? Well, I can tell you that they make the most money when your money is at risk. As a matter of fact, this whole system that they have—beautiful offices around the country and retail brokers who are there to sell things to clients—would not exist if everybody with an account at a big Wall Street firm put his or her money just in CDs and government bonds; there is not enough profit in those products to support that distribution system. They have to have accounts with risk money in it so they can borrow against that money to trade for their own accounts. They also have to have that money at risk so brokers can move it around and generate additional commissions and so they can lend those securities to other parties *who want to bet against your stocks going up.* Sometimes it's even your firm that is betting against your stocks going up. This is why they want your money at risk.

This creates a dilemma, because for most people the day they retire represents a fundamental change in their lives, and it should also represent a fundamental change in their investments. But if you are dealing with a big Wall Street firm, many times instead of making a bigger portion of your money safe, they just simply move it around to different mutual funds.

We discuss in another area of this book the difference between bond funds and stock funds and that bond funds are still risky; nonetheless, when you retire, you just get a bigger allocation of bond mutual funds with most Wall Street firms.

So understand the biases and remember the importance of dealing with independent financial advisors and certified financial planners. I was trained by a big Wall Street firm; we would have certain lists of stocks we were supposed to push, stocks that would make the firm the most money. I can promise you that this still goes on today.

Sometimes there are certain investments that are perfect for a client, but if I work for a certain firm, I cannot necessarily recommend those investments. If I am an employee of a firm, I do not have independence.

It's very important to be aware of the biases that exist in financial magazines and Wall Street firms, but realize that I am not saying to immediately close your account right now—just be aware of those biases. I am also not saying that everybody who works for a big Wall Street firm is bad. I have friends who work for big Wall Street firms, and some of them have been there for up to 28 years. Those firms have them so locked up with pension benefits and deferred compensation plans that they can't leave unless they really want to hurt their families financially, so they are kind of stuck. You can still find a person at those firms who will act in your best interest, but the pressure on brokers at Wall Street firms is very heavy, and there are certain investments and products that they have to recommend.

Let's talk about insurance companies. If you go to an insurance company or somebody who is a "financial advisor" who happens to work for a big insurance company such as MassMutual or MetLife or Northwestern Mutual, chances are that their compensation structure is set up so that the advisor makes the most money by selling you insurance, and you have to understand this. Does this mean that your person at such a company is a bad advisor? No, not necessarily, but you have to understand that there is a system in those companies by which they get paid more money to sell insurance.

Is it important to understand these biases? Yes, it is. Does that mean a person who works for these companies cannot do a good job for you? No; I think some can do a good job for you, but they are few and far between.

The last area I would like to address is a broker who works for a bank. Folks, be very cautious of brokers who work for banks. I have never met one who was a really good advisor, one who could make it on his or her own outside of the bank. I am sure there are a few, but I personally don't know of many.

Having a good and independent financial advisor is very critical because those biases will be removed. Independent financial advisors pay their own bills, and independent financial firms are out on their own to make it in the marketplace. If they are successful, they are probably serving their clients well.

STOCK MARKET HISTORY

Picture this: You have an investment account that is going down; you see that each time you get your statement. The news about the economy is not good, and you're concerned that your account might continue to decline. You tell your broker that you're worried and maybe you should get out of the investments that are going down. What does the broker say to you? You tend to hear things such as, "Hang in there," "The market always comes back," "You're in it for the long run," and "You haven't lost money until you sell." I say *hogwash*, and I'm being polite with my language here.

Let's examine some stock market periods and you judge. Do you want to gamble with your hard-earned retirement money and risk going into one of these periods? Chart 1 shows the Dow Jones Industrial Average from October 1928 to December 1949. Yes, you're reading it correctly. The Dow was at 375 in 1929, and 20 years later it was at 200. Down a total of 47% in 20 years. Now you're saying that that was the Great Depression, an exception. Oh, really? Let's look at Chart 2, the NASDAQ from December 27, 1999, to December 28, 2009. The NASDAQ went from 5,000 to 2,300 in 10 years. How long until it gets back to 5,000? Some people are still in mutual funds that have been affected by this, and they're still hanging onto them, thinking that the NASDAQ is going to magically bounce back, when in effect there are more companies in the NASDAQ now than there were back then.

Now, some compare our present-day economy after the real estate and banking crisis to Japan's in 1990 when that country had its real estate crisis. Let's look at Chart 3. In 1990, the Nikkei, the Japanese equivalent of our Dow, was at 35,000. In December 2009, 19 or 20 years later, it was at around 11,000. That's a total loss of 69% in 20 years.

Last, let's look at the Dow from 1964 to 1982. On Chart 4, you'll notice that the Dow over this 18-year period was basically flat. Also notice that there were five one- to two-year periods during which if you could have caught some of the upside of the Dow and not lost money during the following downturns, you probably could have earned a 7% rate of return during this period as indicated by the lines across the chart.

It's all about protecting principal, folks. The reality is that we have had multiple 15- to 20-year periods in this country when the market and things tied to the stock market did very little. This is why the indexing or passive management philosophy, the theory that you should just buy index funds because no one beats the market, just doesn't work for most people, especially those who need income from their portfolios.

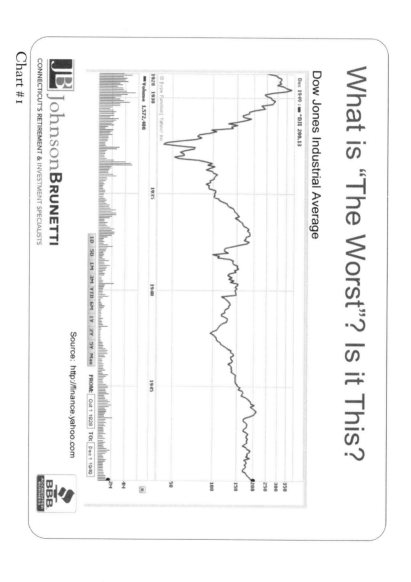

What is "The Worst"? Is it This?

Dow Jones Industrial Average

Chart #1

How About This?

NASDAQ Composite

Week of Dec 14, 2009 : ■ ^IXIC 2,211.6899

© Type Function Yahoo! Inc.

2000   2002   2004   2006   2008

■ Volume 2,112,908,032

5K
4.50K
4K
3.50K
3K
2.50K
2K
1.50K

10B
5B

1D 5D 1M 3M YTD 6M 1Y 2Y 5Y Max   FROM: Dec 27 1999 TO: Dec 28 2009

Source: http://finance.yahoo.com

JB JohnsonBRUNETTI
CONNECTICUT'S RETIREMENT & INVESTMENT SPECIALISTS

Chart #2

Or Maybe This?

Source: http://finance.yahoo.com

JohnsonBrunetti
CONNECTICUT'S RETIREMENT & INVESTMENT SPECIALISTS

Chart #3

Or Even This?

Dow Jones Industrial Average

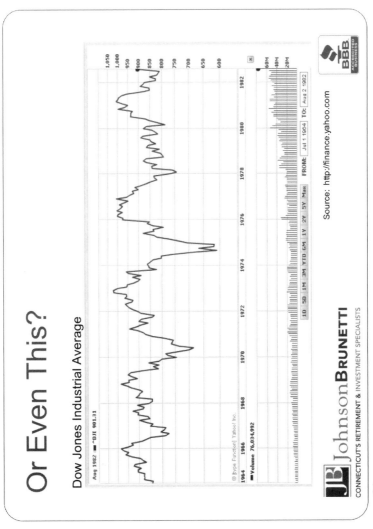

Source: http://finance.yahoo.com

JohnsonBRUNETTI
CONNECTICUT'S RETIREMENT & INVESTMENT SPECIALISTS

Chart #4

My favorite way to position a portfolio for retirement is as follows: notice the circle chart here where you have 1/3 in equities, 1/3 in alternatives and steady income accounts, and 1/3 in safe accounts. The 1/3 in safe accounts utilizes, depending on current rates, government bonds, fixed annuities, indexed annuities, and indexed CDs, in combination for safety and guarantees. This produces a portfolio that offers you peace of mind.

The 1/3 that comprises alternative and steady income investments includes real estate, corporate bonds, preferred stocks, business development companies, private equity type companies, leasing programs, and energy trusts. These steady alternative accounts are designed to spin off a 6% to 8% cash flow with very little fluctuation of principal. The income can be spent or put in other investments for future income needs.

The final 1/3 includes stocks, managed accounts, and mutual funds. The goal here is to grow this third by 10%. But if it doesn't work out that way, then we can provide all our income needs from the safe and steady part of the portfolio.

One last point on this subject: since the biggest concern among retirees in the United States is running out of money, we try to guarantee all of their needed income. Think of it as building your own private pension. The old pensions that are less common today than they were 15 or 20 years ago really worked pretty well. You got a steady check every month. You didn't have to worry about outliving it. You could even have an option that allows your spouse to continue to enjoy that income after your death. Do you know that you can design a private plan that works just like that, and many of these plans will guarantee a 5% or 6% income? With today's innovative financial products, this can be done. That's the good news.

MARKET
Things sensitive to stock market volatility

ALTERNATIVE
Accounts with steady returns regardless of stock market

SAFE
Cannot lose principal or interest earned

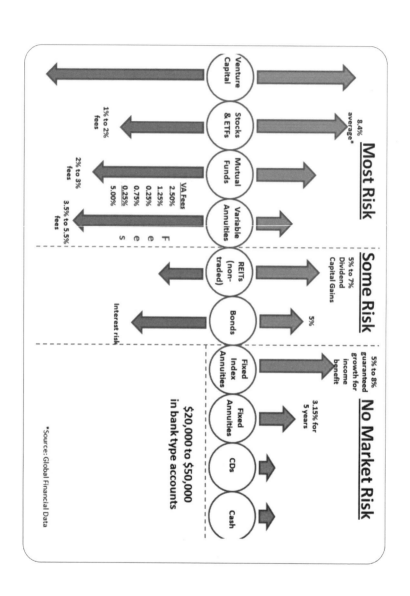

Most Risk

- Venture Capital
- Stocks & ETFs
- Mutual Funds
- Variable Annuities

8.4% average*

1% to 2% fees

2% to 3% fees

VA Fees
2.50% Fees
1.25% Fees
0.25% Fees
0.75% Fees
5.00% Fees

3.5% to 5.5% fees

Some Risk

- REITs (non-traded)
- Bonds

5% to 7%
Dividend
Capital Gains

5%

Interest risk

No Market Risk

- Fixed Index Annuities
- Fixed Annuities
- CDs
- Cash

5% to 8% guaranteed growth for income benefit

3.15% for 5 years

$20,000 to $50,000 in bank type accounts

*Source: Global Financial Data

GREED-ENTITLEMENT-ARROGANCE
THE TRUE CULTURE OF WALL STREET

These are the three core characteristics that permeate Wall Street, and it's really unfortunate. Let's talk about what Wall Street was originally meant to do: to be a stock exchange that allowed companies to raise capital by selling equity or stock in themselves. This is in itself a very noble concept. If my manufacturing company needs money to build a new plant, to expand, or to buy machinery, I can sell equity in my company, perhaps 10, 15, 25, 50%, or even more of it. Investors are able to purchase shares of my company, and I use that money to expand, to increase the value of the company. As the value of the company increases, the value of my ownership goes up, and so does that of the investors.

The second intention of Wall Street was to offer IOUs or bonds in companies. Instead of selling ownership in my company, I can sell IOUs. I can sell a bond and guarantee an investor an interest rate in addition to his principal back at a certain time.

So this was the idea of Wall Street: to raise capital so that businesses could expand and thereby increase their value by borrowing dollars or by selling equity and putting it back into the business, which would generate a higher rate of return than the cost of the capital. So what has happened on Wall Street? Wall Street has turned into a money machine. Those who are insiders, those who are part of the old boys' network if you will (and I say old boys carefully, but it is indeed mostly boys), are in a culture permeated by greed, entitlement, and arrogance.

Let's talk about greed. Think about the mortgage debacle that happened in 2006, 2007, and 2008. People were able to borrow money to buy a house without providing any documentation of income or employment. They could just make up numbers, put them down on a mortgage application, and get a mortgage. This happened because the profit and fees earned by making those loans were much higher than the actual risks. In fact, most of the time there was no risk to the lender because Wall Street was able to package those loans, collect a big fat fee, and then sell them to investors around the world—investors like you and me who had money in pension plans, and other investors including different countries and cities, endowments, and charities that put their money into these mortgage-backed securities or collateralized debt obligations called CMBs or CDOs, and what happened? There was no real value there.

Let's think about who *really* got hurt by the mortgage debacle. Did Wall Street, which financed and created these vehicles, get hurt? Not really. Now you may say their stock prices got hurt, and that's true; they certainly took some losses. But look at the bonuses of the people who packaged and sold these products collected in 2005, 2006, and 2007, before the entire market imploded. Huge, extravagant bonuses. If you're a Wall Street executive who can collect $20 million or $30 million for packaging products that hurt the public, you can focus on the short-term, put the money in your pocket, and not worry about the long term.

Now let me be very clear here. I'm not sure that every executive who packaged those products thought the mortgage market was going to implode, but there were plenty of warning signs, and any time you throw that much money around in the form of commissions and bonuses to people for packaging products that might not have inherent value, you're going to have problems.

Now what we have is an American public whose house values have gone down. Jobs have been lost, and retirements have been postponed. Let's be clear: part of the reason house values have gone down is because their values at the end of 2006 were artificially high because of increased liquidity in the marketplace. But the bottom line is that we feel poorer, the market hurt, most of our 401(k)s went down, but the Wall Street fat cats are still fat.

Will this be the end of it? No, absolutely not. In the late 70s and early 80s, it was junk bonds. After that was the Internet bubble; companies were valued much higher than their real, intrinsic value.

Thankfully, through it all our economy worked, and the market correction was exactly that: a correction. Things were out of line, and that correction was needed. But the greed of Wall Street is something you need to understand. We should be aware of it because it infects your investments—not affects, *infects*—your investments. When you buy mutual funds or stocks, you need to be very aware that you are on a playing field that is stacked against you as an individual investor, and you better be aware of the costs and the fees and the maybe "backdoor" motivations of those producing and selling those products.

Does that mean every product is bad? Absolutely not. We've made a lot of money for our clients in these Wall Street–created products, but you just need to be very careful. Once again, when something seems too good to be true, it probably is. Remember the Lehman Brothers, the Bear Stearns, and the Goldman Sachs.

Let's talk about Goldman Sachs for a minute. I remember reading an article that came out at the beginning of 2011 that said that Goldman Sachs had an investment fund just for the partners of Goldman Sachs. This private fund was offered a big stake in Facebook at a certain price. The partners decided to pass on that stake; they thought that it was overvalued, but they nonetheless turned around and offered it to their institutional clients and investors. Let me say that again: the partners thought it was overvalued, but they offered it to their institutional investors and pocketed huge fees for doing so. You can certainly reference this by searching the article: "Goldman Sachs Passes on Facebook Investment" on Google (2011). The investment offering wasn't good enough for the partners, but it was good enough for the clients. That's a problem, folks.

Now let's talk about this sense of entitlement. What really drives this idea that people can hurt the public by their greed and not have a problem with it? How can they sleep at night? It's simply a sense of entitlement. Because they went to the right schools, because they grew up on the right coast, because they played lacrosse, because they had the right connections, they're entitled to make $3 million, $10 million, $20 million, and more. It's this sense of entitlement as well as greed that really causes a problem on Wall Street. If I feel that I'm entitled to make a ton of money and it doesn't matter how much it hurts you because you just didn't grow up in the right family or go to the right school or attend the right church or synagogue, that's a problem, a problem that hurts all of America. America was built on the backs of workers, and those workers should benefit.

Before I start sounding like a pro-union speaker, let me say that unions have cost us some jobs in this country. They have certainly hurt the auto industry. The unions started because workers were being abused, and a correction to that was in order. However, sometimes things that start out as good go a little too far. Wall Street was started to finance American business but in this case, this entitlement attitude of Wall Street needs to be corrected.

The other attitude that goes along with entitlement is arrogance, the arrogance of somebody standing up and saying that he is entitled to this amount of money because he created these products that fuel America. Well, maybe they do fuel America, but they also can hurt America when greed, entitlement, and arrogance run out of control.

So understand how the culture of Wall Street affects you as an investor. Wall Street is rewarded and makes money when you take risk. When you put your dollars in a Wall Street firm, you can be rewarded or you can be hurt. But make no bones about it folks; that firm makes a lot of money when your money is at risk. If everybody with an account at a big brokerage firm put money solely in CDs or Treasury Bills, do you think Wall Street firms would make enough money to keep their doors open and pay for that fancy office space they have? Absolutely not. So don't expect your broker employed at that big Wall Street firm to make the fundamental change in your portfolio that needs to be made when your retirement comes. That's not going to happen, folks. He's been trained to keep your money at risk.

At your retirement, your money should be safe. Let's be very clear that that's how it affects you, the individual investor—your retirement could be forever ruined.

I realize I've gone off on a bit of a rampage, but I am sick and tired of greed, entitlement, and arrogance, the attitude of Wall Street brokers who feel that they are entitled to pull money out of the workingman's pocket and to not care about the amount of pain and misery they inflict on the innocent and unsuspecting public.

PEOPLE WHO WANT TO TAKE YOUR MONEY

One of the most important considerations in financial planning is not just the rate of return you get on your investments or the security of knowing that your money will last as long as you live; it's keeping your money away from people who want to take it. The purpose of this chapter is to go through some of the different people and entities out there that may want to get their hands on your money and take it from you and spend it in a way that you don't approve of or just simply take it away so you and your family cannot use it.

The first party we think of is the IRS, which is notorious for penalizing people who do the right thing. What do

I mean by that? Well, if you don't save enough money for retirement, you can simply go on Social Security and probably take part in all kinds of state and federal programs to help you pay for your retirement. You certainly don't have to pay for healthcare, one of the most important and costly expenses in retirement. Yet if you do a good job like our clients do in saving for retirement, the IRS is there to take anywhere between 10, 15, 25, maybe as much as *45 cents of every retirement dollar* that you would like to spend. That's right—up to 45 cents when you factor in the taxes on Social Security, income taxes, and state taxes, which we're about to discuss.

TAXES, TAXES, AND MORE TAXES

Let's talk about the different types of taxes. One, of course, is income tax. IRAs are talked about more in the chapter "The Knockout Punch to the Taxman." When you take money out of an IRA or a 401(k), it gets taxed by simply being added to your income. In this situation, you've saved money all your life, and now you begin to spend it. Well, you may have Social Security, you may have a pension, and let's say you take, oh, $1,500 a month or so, $18,000 a year, out of your IRA or 401(k). It's possible that you're going to pay income tax of anywhere between $3,000 and possibly up to $7,000 a year on that money. Think about that; think about how much time you spent trying to get a decent rate of return on your money. Let's say you average 7% over your lifetime. Well, you didn't really get to keep 7%, did you? Because when you take out the money, the IRS gets 33% of it, so you really get only 4.25%. The IRS is very, very happy because all of that time you spent saving in your IRA or 401(k), they were your partner. You just didn't know it then; they were a silent partner until you began taking money out. One of the most important things we can do is be tax-efficient with our investments. So once again, the IRS is there in line from an income tax standpoint.

Let's talk about the estate tax next. Legislation now puts a very high limit on the estate tax. The current federal estate tax only applies to assets over $5.43 million per person (2015). Unless you have a net worth over that amount you don't owe federal estate tax. For most of our clients, this does not apply. Most of them are just good, average, hard-working Americans who did a great job of saving money and have investable assets of less than $2 million. So that's a little bit about the IRS and the money that they want to take from you.

Now let's talk about state governments. In Connecticut, where I live, the state inheritance tax affects estates or net worths above $2 million, while the federal government taxes everything above $5 million. Well, in Connecticut, or anywhere in the northeast in this country, or certainly on the West Coast, it is not very hard to have a net worth over $2 million. If you have $1 million in savings and you live for another 10 years or so in Connecticut and you own your home, chances are that between the value of your home, your pension, your IRAs, your 401(k)s, and your various investments and savings, it'd be very easy to have a net worth of more than $2 million. So this is an area that you need to plan for. Do not allow the state to take more money than they deserve because of improper planning.

Another area that may want to take your money is healthcare, including healthcare insurance companies and health providers and, in particular, nursing homes. *Did you know that there is a 40% chance that one or the other of a married couple older than 65 will spend time in a nursing home?* What does a nursing home cost? Well, I know the one close to my house in central Connecticut charges now approximately $275 per *day*, over $100,000 *per year*. And it's an average nursing home, not a Cadillac by any means. How would a couple pay for that? If somebody has an average amount of investment assets, it would probably leave the spouse who does not need the nursing-home care impoverished by the time his or her spouse in the nursing home died. So it's very important that we plan for this, and there are two ways. One is by buying different types of insurance policies. The good news is that the old long-term care insurance policies that involved paying premiums that we lose if we don't use them are not as popular as they used to be. There is a new and improved type of insurance policy that allows you to set money aside, and if you need nursing home care you have the long-term care insurance and the nursing home insurance, but if you never need the nursing home care, *your family gets all that money back plus a return on the money!* So you want to investigate this new type of hybrid nursing home insurance.

The other important way of planning for elder-care asset protection, and we stress this with all of our clients, is by getting a *proper* attorney as soon as there's an inkling of a problem. And please note my emphasis on the word *proper*. Most attorneys, unfortunately, at least those whom we have come across, will be glad to do work when it comes to asset protection, but they are not necessarily competent to do so. It takes a very strong character for somebody to say, "I can't do this work; I'm in over my head," as opposed to just collecting a fee. Well, the good news is that here in Connecticut and across the country we know of a good network of high-quality elder-care attorneys who can protect your assets.

Now someone might say, "Wait a minute, Joel! Isn't there a five-year look-back if I give assets away within five years of going into a nursing home that the government takes back?" Well, that's not exactly the way it works. That's why it's so important to educate yourself on these subjects. We can help you, and good elder-care attorneys can help you, but make sure you pick the right one and you get references. We have a network of such attorneys with whom we're very pleased. One of the attorneys we know who works very close to our office just won a court case against the State of Connecticut, which was trying to recapture assets that his client had given away and put into an annuity before going into a nursing home. And so the good news is there are competent professionals out there.

The next group of people who may want to get your money are the people your kids have married. Now let's face it, moms and dads; we all love our kids, but sometimes we're not too sure about the people they marry. There could be a divorce, there could be a situation in which we leave money to our son, for instance, when we die, and then our son dies and his wife remarries. All of a sudden, the money we wanted to go to our child and our grandchildren ends up part of another marriage and possibly not getting to our grandchildren at all, or getting spread out among people who are not even in our bloodline. This is why it's so very, very important to work with a competent financial planner who works within a network or a team of attorneys who can help you structure your estate so that this can never happen.

Has anybody ever told you that you can control these things from the grave? The wonderful thing about a trust, if a trust is appropriate for you, is that you get to write the rules, and almost any rule that you want to impose either on your children or the people your children marry can be imposed. What we're talking about here is not trying to punish other people, not trying to be vindictive; what we're talking about here is good stewardship. *You've earned your money, you have certain values when it comes to money, and you deserve to have those values expressed, even when you're no longer here, and maybe for one, two, or three generations to come.* This can be done when it comes to your money. It's just a matter of proper estate planning.

Now let's talk about one other thing that I'm going to illustrate with a story. My family was recently on vacation in the Canadian Rockies and having a wonderful time. It's absolutely gorgeous scenery. In fact, the scenery is so stunning that at times when we would look out our hotel window or go for a walk and look up at the mountains, they almost didn't seem real because they were just so vivid, the air was so crisp, and the sky and the lakes were unbelievable. Well, there's also a lot of wildlife up there, bears, moose, and deer. We were having a wonderful time when one morning my 11-year-old Noah pulled me by the arm through the lobby and outside the hotel. He was so excited that I thought for sure he had seen a bear or a deer or elk and was going to show it to me. He's a real animal lover. Well, what does he see out in front of the hotel? A $280,000 Lamborghini, a car that'll go 220 miles an hour. Noah wanted his picture taken in front of that car. I'm no dummy. He loves cars, my oldest son likes cars, and I like cars too. But the last thing I want is for him to blow his inheritance on one or two of those cars after my wife and I pass away. We all know that sometimes our kids don't share our values with money. And so with Noah, if he continues his love of cars, if he continues to spend his allowance as quickly as he does on things like candy and so on, well, we might just put a provision in our will and in our trust that says he doesn't get a lump sum but perhaps a certain stipend every month for as long as he lives, and there would be other money available for certain things, like education or charitable giving. You can do this; it's control from the grave. The important thing is that you have certain values when it comes to your money, values that you want expressed in your estate plan.

One last little statistic I want to share with you, and this is so, so important for you to understand: most of the time, after both spouses die, their kids learn that their parents' IRA is cashed out completely. *The average inheritance in this country is spent within nine months.* Think about that when you plan your estate. Once again, do you have good kids or bad kids or both? I don't mean good or evil kids; I mean kids who are good with money and kids who are bad with money. Many of us have children who have challenges in life, and maybe there's a need to restrict some of those kids from getting money.

One more circumstance we see in our financial services practice: many of our clients have children with special needs. Sometimes it's a matter of severe retardation; other times it might be a form of autism; still other times it might be some sort of traumatic injury for which a child is getting some type of state aid. Generally, if somebody getting state aid inherits money, that event will disqualify them for that aid. The inheritance has to be spent on their care before they can go back on state aid. Hence the need for special-needs planning, a very, very critical matter. You can keep a special-needs child from being disqualified for state aid by setting up a special-needs trust. We've set up such trusts many times with the assistance of the attorneys in our network; this is a way you can make sure that a special-needs child is taken care of, that the inheritance is split equally and cannot be taken by the state.

This has been a chapter that talked briefly about some of the people who want to take your money. Folks, your money is *your* money; you should be able to control it and decide where it gets spent.

THE TRUTH ABOUT MUTUAL FUNDS

Do you know the number-one way that Americans save for retirement and the number-one way that Americans invest while in retirement? You guessed it—mutual funds. Are mutual funds good or bad? Well, they're better than some alternatives, but there are some facts that can make mutual funds very problematic to own.

Deferred compensation plans, 401(k)s, 403(b)s, and even brokerage accounts are full of mutual funds that many advisors use to invest for clients, and these funds can be good or bad. How do you know that you have a good one? Do you know that 85% of mutual funds according to Morningstar did not beat the benchmark that they are measured against? Eighty-five percent. This means that out of the 10,000-plus mutual funds that existed in the beginning of 2011, 15% are good and 85% are lousy. What are the chances that you have a good mutual fund?

We're going to explore in this chapter the problem with mutual funds, when they should be used and when they should not be used. To be clear—full disclosure here—we use mutual funds in some of the portfolios we manage for our retirement clients, but I am very careful to select mutual funds that meet very stringent criteria that we developed at our firm. Here, however, is the problem: some advisors use mutual funds exclusively, and mutual funds have very high expenses. Some of you are saying, "Well, I can buy a Vanguard fund for instance, an index fund that charges only five basis points, 1/20th of a percent, in expenses, maybe 1/10th of a percent in expenses. That's a very low expense, Joel." That's correct; that's a very low expense, but index funds in my opinion can do fine in certain types of markets but very poorly in others. If you bought index funds and you followed the indexing philosophy of John Bogel, Vanguard's former chairman, how did you do in 2008? Come on—how did you do? If you had the Index 500 fund in 2008, your money was down approximately 35% to 40%!

Now if you buy actively managed funds (of which I am a bit more of a fan), then you have other issues. One is that the expenses are much higher—1%, possibly 2%, in management fees. In addition to that are all kinds of other expenses not disclosed in the prospectuses because they are expenses of custody and trading and other costs. Our firm uses a special analysis tool that gets to the root of what you're really paying, and you'd be surprised. Mutual funds say they have a 1% expense ratio, but when analyzed and all the other costs are backed out, many times the cost of owning that fund is as high as 5%, and we've seen even 6% per year. I was shocked when, 16 years ago, I owned a mutual fund that after additional research I discovered had expenses of 6.5% per year. What it means, folks, is that if you had $100,000 in it, the market had to go up 6%, $6,000, before you even broke even because of those expenses. These very high expenses and trading costs are one of the problems of mutual funds.

The second big problem with mutual funds is that the money managers don't get paid for performance but for the amount of assets they attract. Let me say that again: they do not necessarily get paid for performance, but they do get paid for the amount of assets they attract. Money managers of most mutual fund families are paid a certain percentage, typically 0.25% of the total assets under management. So instead of having the incentive to beat the market, they have the incentive to attract more dollars. This is why you see companies such as Fidelity, Vanguard, and T. Rowe Price doing so much advertising and marketing. It's all about attracting dollars, folks. So keep that in mind, the compensation structure in most mutual funds families may be rewarding the wrong outcome.

There are certain mutual fund families that I think really have it right when it comes to this compensation issue because they reward their managers for long-term performance, but please understand that attracting dollars to a mutual fund sometimes pays a lot more than making dollars in the market.

I was recently at an investment conference at which one speaker was a personal friend of the manager of one of the most popular mutual funds held in retirement plans. It's a fairly large mutual fund with approximately $40 billion under management. The gentleman speaking, who is a friend of mine, was curious to how long it took a money manager to take a reasonable position in a stock. As some of you know, mutual funds will typically take about 1% to 2% of their money and buy into a stock if the managers have a strong conviction about its value. They obviously want to have enough of the stock so that if the stock moves up it will have a positive effect on the mutual fund, but if the stock does not work out, the loss does not ruin the performance of the entire fund. Well, my friend asked this world-class money manager how long it took to build that 1% to 2% position for his mutual fund. I was shocked at the answer: anywhere from 6 to 10 weeks. What that means is if a money manager wants to take a position in a stock because he believes in the company, he can't just buy enough stock to have a significant, positive impact on his fund in one day as you and I could. It takes him up to 10 weeks to build such a position in that stock because if he takes 1% to 2% of his fund's money and buys that stock in one day, he could move that stock up substantially, possibly out of the price range where he wants to own it. Think about how much can change, folks, in 6 to 10 weeks. This is a significant problem with popular funds; it can take far too long for a money manager to take certain positions in some stocks.

Let's think about the opposite of that. What if there's bad news about a company that makes a money manager want to get out of the company? That also might take 6 to 10 weeks. We saw an example of this in the dot com bubble; when it began to burst, people were pulling money out of Janus, a big mutual fund company. When Janus started selling its positions, it actually drove the market down because it had such a huge share of technology stocks. A mutual fund's size can affect its ability to sell as well as buy, and either can be problematic.

On the following few pages is some research I've collected from the personalfunds.com website. For the sake of fairness, you might be reading this book a year or two after we did this research, so I haven't mentioned the names of the funds, but I have mentioned the companies. What I offer is analysis of mutual funds from mutual fund companies such as BlackRock, AIM, Fidelity, Oppenheimer, and Janus, some of the most popular. I have written down the cost of owning some of their best-performing funds, which range anywhere from 1.7% and 2.5%, in the case of one of the funds. This gets very expensive. If you look at the prospectuses of some of these funds, it shows that you're paying only 0.88%, but in reality you're actually paying up to 2.47% in the most expensive of the funds.

Let's talk about good mutual funds, because I mentioned earlier that we use certain mutual funds in some of our managed portfolios. I like mutual funds that allow me to bet on the manager rather than on the particular fund or fund company. I know of one fund we use in many of our portfolios whose money manager has a certain style; he owns only about 20 to 22 stocks, and he's got a tremendous track record; the fund does not restrict what types of companies he can own, so he can own international or U.S. companies, he can own growth companies, he can own real estate companies, and he can own large or small companies. He can go just about wherever he wants that fits his investment style. So what we really do here is buy a money manager and allow him to do what he does best.

There's another fund we use to anchor our portfolios that specializes in stocks that pay dividends and has tremendous protection against down markets. We love this particular fund because it pays dividends of up to 4%, which provides a nice income stream for those who want that. And over the long haul it has returned another 5% to 8% above those dividends. If we look at this fund from 2000 to 2010, a time during which the Standard & Poor's 500 actually lost money, this fund earned 7.5% total return, and if you took your dividends out, it still remained positive at about 3% per year in addition to the dividends. That's 7% to 7.5% per year over a 10-year period that was a down market, a very positive return for a stock fund. These are the types of things that we look for in mutual funds.

We cannot even buy into the funds of some of the best-performing managers because the minimum investment required can start at $5 million. These are commonly referred to as hedge funds, although they don't always hedge in the classic sense. However, some of these money managers charge up to 3% of the fund's assets, plus transaction costs, plus a certain percentage of the profits. So if a fund has a total return of 20% in a year, you could pay anywhere between 6% and 7% to own that manager. I repeat: 6% to 7%. Why do the wealthiest people put money with these money managers? Because it's not about the cost; it's about the return.

Be aware of how expensive mutual funds can be, but then keep their costs in perspective: *Sometimes you get what you pay for.*

WHY REAL ESTATE WORKS

In this chapter we'll address how and why real estate investing works. One of the reasons real estate works is that everyone needs somewhere to live and somewhere to work. You buy a house because chances are you don't want to sleep out on the streets. Well, there is a value in that home; it's residential real estate. If you own an apartment building, you rent out those apartments and in so doing you create value. What other kinds of real estate are there? How about office buildings? And consider warehouses, where companies store goods waiting to be sold.

Another reason why real estate works is that we're not making any more land. There is a limited supply of land.

A third reason that real estate works is that I can rent property and create cash flow. For example, if I spend $1 million on an apartment building I can create perhaps a 12% cash flow with the rent. If it costs me only 4% to operate the building, then I pocket 8%. *You* do the math. Even if it costs me 6% to operate the building, I pocket a very nice 6% cash flow.

Last but not least, real estate purchased for the right price keeps up with inflation. If my apartment building appreciates by 3% to 4% per year, I'm keeping up with inflation. When I sell that building someday, I'm going to get that much more than I put in, and I enjoyed the cash flow in the meantime. So these are some of the reasons why real estate works. Much of the wealth in our country was created through real estate. Consider railroads, for instance; a tremendous amount of the share value of publicly traded railroads is due to the real estate they hold.

People such as Donald Trump—whether you like him or not—have made money buying and developing real estate. I have clients who are real estate developers who buy a piece of land, build and sell 12 houses, and make—if they do it correctly and well—a very, very nice profit. Real estate can offer tremendous returns on equity.

The other factor that makes real estate work is that we don't need to come up with all the cash to buy it. If I want to buy $1 million of General Electric stock today, I have to come up with $500,000 and borrow the other half (and pay interest on that) in order to control $1 million of General Electric shares. With real estate, I can put up 20%, sometimes less than that, in effect controlling $1 million worth of real estate for $200,000 or less. This gives me tremendous leverage. If that $1 million piece of real estate I'm controlling for $200,000 goes up 5% in value, the increase on my $200,000 is $50,000, a 25% return. You have to factor in interest rate costs here, but I think you get the idea, folks. I talk about in some of my seminars how real estate investment trusts, which are basically funds of many different real estate properties, can generate a 6% to 7% yield plus the value of inflation growth.

A fourth reason real estate works is that it can be an inflation hedge. Let's say inflation runs at 4%. If I can get 6% or 7% from an investment plus 4% per year on the back end, that's a tremendous value. I'm talking about a 9%, 10%, even an 11% rate of return. Sounds pretty good. Why doesn't everybody do it? Well, let's talk about that. Real estate is not liquid, is it? That can be good, but it can also be bad. If your money is in real estate and you need cash today, you might not be able to sell your real estate except at a low price, perhaps a price much less than the real value of that property. Investing in real estate causes you to give up liquidity in order to get stability and a rate of return, a principle that we've talked about in other sections of this book. If you're willing to give up liquidity, you can create tremendous value with real estate.

You want to be very careful to make sure, however, that you have enough liquidity to meet emergency needs, for instance, if the bank calls that loan or if interest rates spike and yours is an adjustable-rate loan. There are many ins and outs of real estate. The purpose of this chapter is not to show you how to make money in real estate—there are plenty of books that do that. What the purpose of this book is for is to point out different ways that money works. And certainly real estate works in a very advantageous way.

ONCE AGAIN, JUST TO REVIEW:

• Everybody needs somewhere to live and somewhere to work.

• They're not making any more land.

• If I own real estate, I can take out a very nice cash flow.

- Real estate purchased for the right price is a great inflation hedge.

Keep in mind that the real estate trusts we talked about, if purchased correctly and cautiously, can create a very nice stream of income while increasing in value at the rate of inflation.

20-year Annualized Returns by Asset Class (1990-2009)

Asset	Return
REITs	9.90%
S&P 500	8.20%
Bonds	7.00%
Oil	6.70%
Gold	5.20%
EAFE	4.40%
Homes	3.20%
Inflation	2.80%
Average Investor	2.30%

Indexes used are as follows: REITs: NAREIT Equity REIT Index; EAFE: MSCI EAFE; Oil: WTI Index; Bonds: Barclays Capital U.S. Aggregate Index; Homes: median sales price of existing single-family homes; Gold: USD/troy oz.; Inflation: CPI. Average asset allocation investor return is based on an analysis by Dalbar Inc. which utilizes the net of aggregate mutual fund sales, redemptions and exchanges each month as a measure of investor behavior. Returns are annualized (and total return where applicable) and represent the 20-year period ending 12/31/09 to match Dalbar's most recent analysis.

Example of Real Estate Returns Compared to Other Assets

THE ONE-PAGE ROADMAP FOR YOUR FINANCES

Have you ever read a financial plan prepared by a broker who works for a large financial firm such as Merrill Lynch, Ameriprise, UBS, MetLife, or the like? These plans come in a big binder, are at least 80-plus pages long, and are very complicated. You know what happens when the prospective client takes these plans home after sitting for up to two hours going over the plan with the broker? Usually nothing.

The plan, too overwhelming for the client, doesn't get implemented. Why is this? It's just too much to do at once. In my 20-plus years of experience in the business of helping people make financial decisions, I have learned that for most of my clients, the best approach is to identify and solve one problem at a time. This is a much simpler approach. It benefits the clients in that most of them find it much easier to move forward.

The typical financial consultant who works for a large institution has been trained to put the whole plan together and present it at one time. They will say that the way I do things is "incomplete, malpractice, or just a way to create a number of financial transactions to get the client involved in."

Let's say you have the perfect financial plan written by two Ivy League PhDs who have 20-plus years of experience on Wall Street. The plan is on beautiful linen paper and presented in a beautiful leather binder. It has every possible contingency in life accounted for: retirement, college funding, special needs for grandkids, insurance planning, and tax planning. But *what good is the plan if it's too overwhelming for the client to implement?* My firm's one-page plan, the Money Map, if you will, helps alleviate this issue. It prompts a discussion about what's most important to the client, who is then able to choose which problem to solve first. Does every life problem get solved? Well, sometimes yes, sometimes no, but if we just solve the top three issues, in 95% of the cases we've done a better job than the broker who uses a complicated plan.

Let me tell you a little secret about the big plan put out by the big firm: Usually it's just a tool to impress the client; what the broker really wants to do is direct the conversation away from it as soon as possible so he can focus on selling you some type of financial product, whether it's mutual funds or insurance, so they can make their commission. They really don't care that much about the plan itself.

I think we've talked enough about what's wrong with the way the other guys do things. I like to stay as positive as possible here. These are the advantages of a SIMPLE plan:

- I get agreement on the problems to be addressed right away. It's up to the client to identify the most important problems. It's not about me and what I think is most important—I want to talk about what concerns the client has and address those problems first.

- Understanding is created because it is visual. Most people think in pictures. Therefore, the simple one-page plan gives people a roadmap, if you will, and a step-by-step process of what to address.

- Investment concepts are simplified for clients. For the first time, the disinterested spouse is not only engaged but also understands how investments work and so takes part in the process.

- By doing things one step at a time, decisions are simple and easy, and therefore the client situation is improved quickly. Everybody wins.

You would think that everyone in the business of giving investment advice would follow this simple approach to helping the public. Wouldn't you? Well, that's not what is happening out there. Most advisors talk in financial jargon, confuse the client, exclude the spouse who is less educated or less interested in investments while trying to prove how smart they are. That process is broken. That process is not about the client at all but about how great the brokerage firm is and how smart the advisor is.

This is *wrong!* The process should be about the clients, their needs, and their goals. Once again, Wall Street has it backwards.

Each chapter in this book can be taken by itself to improve one area of your financial life. You do not need to read the entire book before you take action steps. How do you eat an elephant? One bite at a time. How do you secure your financial future? One step at a time. You will see the progress, feel peace of mind, and be encouraged to continue to take the next step. Remember, it's about progress, not perfection. You don't arrive at the utopia of a perfect financial life. Instead, you arrive at a place where your financial life is a reflection of your goals and values and an example to those you love and influence. Accept the fact that it won't be perfect, but by taking one step at a time and following the Money Map, by implementing our one-page plan, step by step things get better, and you gain peace of mind and purpose with your finances.

Johnson Brunetti
CONNECTICUT'S RETIREMENT & INVESTMENT SPECIALISTS

Income	Income	Tax Deferred	TAX	Tax Deferred	TAX
Pension	**Soc. Sec.**	529/American Mutual Funds Jeremy	Bank $ s BofA	MetLife Fixed @ 5.25% Betty	Commonwealth IBM Trust
$2,478	$36	$54,409	$120,000	$52,625	$441,794
		grandson		expires 12/15/11 Keep	Keep

ROTH IRA	Tax Deferred	ROTH IRA	Tax Deferred	
American Mutual Funds Kate	529/American Mutual Funds Kate	American Mutual Funds Donna	Hartford Variable Annuity	
$9,310	$49,565	$26,476	$158,132	$134,622.20
granddaughter	granddaughter	daughter	Net $134,622.20	

Tax Deferred
Index Annuity 20% Bonus Trust
$161,547
Endurance Plus

Tax Defer

Max Market Risk:	**30%**
Current Market Risk:	57%
Desired Market Risk:	___%

Needs:

Net Worth (excluding primary residence): $1,802,477

Check Beneficiaries
Change advisor
Hartford Payout
ACAT Stock
ROTH Conversion
Bypass trust -- IBM/Annuity
Reduce Mkt exposure to Ret $
Move from Passive Mgt to Active
Growth without Risk
LTC Insurance

Reduce Exposure to Tax
 - Tax Deferred
 - Tax Credit
 - Tax Favored
 - Cap Gain Offset

Marital Trust should r/c 50% of Bill's estate -- CPA is Mr. Jones, West Hartford

Betty Smith

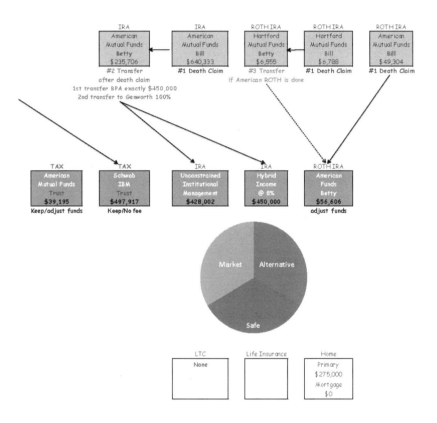

IRA	IRA	ROTH IRA	ROTH IRA	ROTH IRA
American Mutual Funds Betty $235,706	American Mutual Funds Bill $640,333	Hartford Mutual Funds Betty $6,555	Hartford Mutual Funds Bill $6,788	American Mutual Funds Bill $49,304
#2 Transfer after death claim 1st transfer BPA exactly $450,000 2nd transfer to Genworth 100%	#1 Death Claim	#3 Transfer if American ROTH is done	#1 Death Claim	#1 Death Claim

TAX	TAX	IRA	IRA	ROTH IRA
American Mutual Funds Trust $39,195	Schwab IBM Trust $497,917	Unconstrained Institutional Management $428,002	Hybrid Income @ 8% $450,000	American Funds Betty $56,606
Keep/adjust funds	Keep/No fee			adjust funds

Market   **Alternative**   **Safe**

LTC	Life Insurance	Home
None		Primary $275,000 Mortgage $0

COMPONENTS OF YOUR MONEY MAP

You can create your own Money Map that will allow you to visualize your current financial situation. You will need the help of a Money Map professional advisor to recommend changes to fix your personal financial problems.

Let's start by looking at our example of the Money Map on pages 72 and 73. In our example, the husband, Bill, has just passed away. Starting with Social Security and any pensions in the upper left-hand corner, you can see that the client, Betty, in our example, has $2,478 of pension income and $36 of Social Security income each month. The Social Security number is very low because she was a teacher, and teachers in some states are subject to what's called a windfall penalty.

The dark gray boxes on the top left side our Money Map consist of accounts set up by Betty but are accounts that really benefit other people, hence they are blue. These 529 plans are college savings plans, and the Roth IRAs were actually funded by Betty for her grandchildren. The other accounts on the top left of the Smith's plan include $120,000 of bank money and $52,625 in a fixed annuity earning 5.25% interest, and a tax-deferred variable annuity with a $158,132 death benefit that we are recommending replacing, and $441,794 of IBM stock (both light gray).

The reason the IBM stock box and the variable annuity box are light gray is because they have been moved to better accounts. Now, shift over to the top right side of our Money Map for the Smiths. Here we have all the IRA and Roth IRA accounts, which are tax-deferred accounts, and they are all mutual fund accounts in this example. The first step to building your own Money Map is to list straight across the top of your page all of your different accounts. As is the case with Betty's map, I recommend taxable accounts grouped together, tax-deferred accounts grouped as well, and then IRAs, 401(k)s, Roth IRAs, et cetera. From time to time we have clients who have so many accounts that they need a second row of boxes under the top row to list everything. If this is your situation, then you may have overcomplicated your financial life. Be careful—simple is better.

On the bottom right we list properties used for personal use and insurance. You can see in our example that Betty has a house worth $275,000 with no mortgage. She has zero life insurance and zero long-term care insurance. If she had investment properties, they would be represented by boxes up above, since they are investment assets and not personal assets.

Just above the home and the insurance boxes is our pie with the three simple categories of investments that we try to break things down into: "Safe" consists of CDs, cash, fixed annuities, and fixed indexed annuities. "Market" is made up of stocks and mutual funds, managed money accounts, and exchange-traded funds. "Alternative" includes real estate trusts, preferred stocks, managed futures, leasing programs, oil and gas investments, and business development companies or BDCs, which are pools of private floating-rate debt. The purpose of the alternative investment part of the pie is to provide a steady income stream of 6% to 9%; however, this slice is not guaranteed. Alternatives also provide an inflation hedge. The safe part of the pie is fully guaranteed and can also be accessed for income. The market part of the pie is going to have the most fluctuation in value and therefore should not be relied upon for lifestyle or basic needs. The market slice could have investments that could go up 40% or more per year, but those same investments could be down sharply. At my firm we carefully select companies and products that have a proven success record of protecting against the downside.

The bubble chart on the left side of your Money Map is a significant way to contrast the two ways to get better rates of return on investments. Note the three bubbles: safety, growth, and liquidity. These three categories are one of the most important yet overlooked concepts in investing. It is similar to a retail store I once walked into. The store had a sign on the front door that reads, "Highest Quality, Great Service, Lowest Prices—Pick Two." Of the three ingredients—safety, growth, and liquidity—you can have only two in any given investment.

Here's another way to think of this: there are only two ways to increase growth or rate of return in our world: give up safety or give up liquidity, that is, take more risk or make a longer time commitment. Those are the only two ways to increase rate of return.

Money in a bank account offers safety and liquidity but no growth. CDs require us to make a time commitment or give up some liquidity in return for a higher rate of return. Still not a very good rate of return, but the longer time commitment increases the rate of return. It's the same with a fixed annuity. If we make a time commitment of say three to six years, under a normal interest rate environment we will get about 4% to 6% on our money with safety of principal. Stocks or mutual funds offer instant or almost instant liquidity any day the stock exchanges are open. But since we have instant liquidity, we really have no safety; we've given that up to increase rate of return.

What investments offer growth and safety? Well, real estate is one, and others include equipment leasing programs, indexed CDs, and indexed annuities. Real estate is safer than mutual funds and stocks, and so are leasing programs. Indexed annuities and indexed CDs represent true, guaranteed safety. One could also put government bonds in the safety category, but with government bonds we have very little inflation hedge.

Our bubble chart on the left side of the Money Map ties in with the pie chart on the right of the Money Map. Here we illustrate a portfolio made up of the three components:

Market, which is stocks, mutual funds, and ETFs (an ETF, or Exchange Traded Fund, is similar to a mutual fund but less expensive and more tax efficient. You can also sell an ETF anytime throughout the day, unlike a mutual fund).

Alternative, which is made up of assets that produce steady income with a higher degree of safety such as real estate, corporate bonds, preferred stocks, leasing and master limited partnerships.

Safety, which includes CDs, fixed annuities, and treasuries. Each of these slices correlates to our three choices represented by the bubble chart. A good portfolio consists of all three components.

IT'S ALL ABOUT INCOME

Most people stumble through life not knowing what they really want or need.—Joel Johnson

What is retirement planning? It has many definitions. For the purpose of this book I will define retirement planning as defining how your ideal life looks after you no longer have to work, and then making a plan to get to this ideal.

I want you to notice a few key points in the definition. First, there is no age associated with retirement. The most fulfilled people I know, some of whom are 65, 70, even 75, are people still making a significant contribution to others. In fact, you could say that they haven't retired. So let's define retirement as the age at which someone *could* retire but may choose to continue working. For some, that may be working at a company, or consulting, or volunteering somewhere, but they are still active. So now that we know that there is no specific age related to our definition, let's talk about the other important components to this unconventional description of retirement.

The second aspect is freedom. We no longer need to work at a job to earn money, but we may choose to work to earn money. We'll come back to this later.

Third, it is important to know with clarity what you want this stage of your life to look like. Do you want to see your children and grandchildren every week? Do you want to travel frequently? Where will you live? What country will you live in? Will you do the yardwork? See all the possibilities here? Start with a clean slate and create your ideal life.

Here's the most important question: What are all these dreams dependent on besides your health? You've got it—money. But wait; the answer isn't just *money*. That's too simplistic, too vague. The answer is *income*. You need steady, predictable income that will meet all your needs. Why is it important to think this way?

Because I have seen investment portfolios that have been managed poorly and have created insecurity, uncertainty, and anxiety for clients. You can imagine how this affects retirement; you're always a little worried, a little anxious that your money may run out.

My firm, on the other hand, creates investment portfolios designed to produce predictable income, contingency or emergency money, and growth to protect against inflation. We also strive to find products and investments that will guarantee the income clients need so they don't have to worry and can concentrate on their ideal life.

Can this be done? Well, if you have saved enough money, it can be, but you must avoid the mixed messages and erroneous information coming out of the brokerage firms and the mutual fund industry. We've been brainwashed against the very products and investments that can create this predictable income. Let's take the mutual fund industry: go on a mutual fund website and see how much income they say you should take out of a retirement portfolio every year. Most say 4%. Wow. That's pretty low. But they're probably thinking of mutual funds, which explains why they're scared of saying you should take more than 4%. This begs the question: Okay Mr. Schwab, Mr. Fidelity, Mr. T. Rowe

Price, or Mr. Vanguard, you guarantee that as long as I don't take more than 4% from my investments I won't run out of money, correct? No. They won't guarantee anything. In fact, some will say based on a Monte Carlo analysis (an overly complex mathematical analysis based on millions of probable outcomes) that there is a probability that you will run out of money. That's horrible. A 4% cash flow and you still may run out of money? You need $1 million to create a lousy $40,000 of income, and even that's not guaranteed.

Let's talk about the investments you're supposed to avoid at all costs. You know, the ones that the brokers say are costly rip-offs with high fees and commissions, the ones the brokerage firms bash and the mutual fund companies bash, those that other short-sighted talking heads slam. For instance, let's take annuities. There, I said it—those annuities that we've been told not to buy, to stay away from because they're horrible. What's an annuity? It is a tool that can guarantee income, one that, if properly designed by an expert, can guarantee you 5% to 6% income for the rest of your life with no potential for running out of money, and also with potential raises.

You say, "Wait, Joel—6%?"

Yes, 6%, with a guarantee. It's really interesting that the very same mutual fund companies that say annuities are bad cannot guarantee a 6% return. In fact, they can't even guarantee a 4% return. And the insurance company that the brokerage firms, mutual funds, and some uneducated industry pundits warn you to stay away from can guarantee you that 6% income. Gee, I wonder why those firms hate annuities? I'll leave you to figure that out.

Let's talk about another way to get guaranteed income. Some say bond funds. No, no, *no*. There is a use for bond funds. I use them from time to time, but there is a much better way to create income. Guaranteed income, you ask me? Well, you tell me when I'm done explaining.

Pick some American or international companies that you think will not go out of business before you die. Who are they? I'm 48, so let me pick a few for myself that I don't think will go out of business before I die: General Electric, Walmart, Exxon Mobil, Shell Oil, Chevron, Prudential Insurance, MetLife, Google, Apple, Wells Fargo, JPMorgan, and Goldman Sachs—you get the idea. Do you know that right now Wells Fargo bonds are paying between 5% to 7%? This means that if I put a portion of my money with

Wells Fargo, they will guarantee me, for example, 5% to 7% interest for 10 to 20 years. The only way I lose that money is if Wells Fargo breaks its guarantee and is forced into bankruptcy. I just don't think that will happen. As long as Wells Fargo stays out of bankruptcy, I get my 5% to 7%, whatever the current yield was when I bought the bond. Furthermore, my principal is guaranteed by Wells Fargo.

You know, what if I used a combination of bonds from the companies I listed previously? I could create a 6% yield and have my money guaranteed by those particular companies.

How about a combination of annuities and bonds? I can design the annuities to give me raises for my inflation protection and use the bonds for a slightly higher but nonetheless level income. Are you getting the picture here? Could this be something that Wall Street doesn't want to seem better than its prepackaged products that they make so much profit on? Once again, you decide.

Now, before we move on to the next income-producing product, let me say that you should consult an expert before doing this yourself, because one misstep and you'll be stuck with something that could hurt you in the long run. Pay someone 1% to 1.25% and let them be on the hook to create your portfolio for you. It will be well worth it. Those who want to save the 1% to 1.25% by doing it themselves are playing in a game that they just don't understand. In fact, they don't even know who their real competitors are. It's a little bit like a high school football team going out on the field to face the Chicago Bears or the Green Bay Packers. Let me know how it goes next time you decide to operate on yourself to save that small fee you would've paid the doctor, the expert. I think you get the idea here.

Last but not least, let's talk about real estate. Now, we cover why real estate works in another chapter, but for now, just ponder this. You can buy a real estate investment trust that will create 6% to 7% income for you and give you inflation protection. Once again be careful and use an expert, but consider what we've said so far in this chapter.

- Define your ideal retirement using my definition.

- Understand that it's all about the income.

- With the tools I've mentioned, here is the choice: Give a Wall Street firm $1 million and listen when they tell you that you should take $40,000 a year out; you still might run out of money. On the other hand, give Joel or another strong financial professional that $1 million; a properly structured plan will give you $60,000 a year in income and possibly a guarantee of never running out of money if the right products are used. The $60,000 is a 50% raise over the $40,000. Which would you rather have? Folks, as you can see, in retirement planning *it's all about income.*

INVESTMENTS DESIGNED TO PRODUCE INCOME

In this chapter we'll discuss securities and other financial products that produce a steady, predictable income that are for the most part ignored by the major Wall Street firms. Don't get me wrong. My firm reviews clients' statements when they come to get that second opinion from us, and many times we see portfolios with some of these securities that are being used the proper way. However, many other times we see a portfolio of mutual funds created by brokers trying to produce everything, including income with those funds, and really missing the boat as far as safety and predictability are concerned.

Let's discuss securities that produce that steady income most of our retired clients are looking for. Please also note that just because a security is an income-based security or product, it does not mean somebody has to take the income. Many of our clients like these products because they simply produce a nice cash flow of between 5% to 7% or even 8% without excessive fluctuation in principal.

The first security we'll talk about is the corporate bond, many of which are readily available to investors. To keep things simple here, a bond is simply a company's IOU. In the case of a corporate bond, your money is as safe as the company's promise to pay and its stability. In my opinion, an IOU from a strong blue chip company like a General Electric, AT&T, JPMorgan, or some other strong financial institution is a pretty solid promise to pay. I'm 48 years old as I write this, and I don't believe that a company such as General Electric or JPMorgan—or other companies of that caliber—will go out of business before I die. If I can pick up a JP Morgan IOU that says it will pay me 5% or 6% interest for the next five to ten years, and on top of that get all my principal back at the end of that time, I feel pretty confident.

I reviewed some of our portfolios while preparing to write this chapter and saw that we have many bonds in client portfolios that are still paying over 4.5% interest, a very healthy interest rate in this current environment, when 10-year U.S. Treasury bonds are paying in the 2-3% range.

Speaking of U.S. Treasuries, I want people to understand that you can lose money with United States bonds. If you buy a 10-year U.S. Treasury bond today, which is a promise to pay from the US Government, it pays 2.4% interest (the rate as I write this). But if interest rates climb—let's say they climb 2%—new treasuries would be paying 5.4%. Do you think that a 3.4% treasury bond is worth as much as one that pays 5.4%? Of course not. The 3.4% bond's value goes down. If you have to sell it bond before it matures, guess what? It is now worth only about eighty cents on the dollar. That's right; you can lose 20% of your money in a U.S. Treasury bond. The only way to get all you money back is to hold that bond until maturity. You have to be very careful.

In my opinion, the treasury is not a good deal when compared to bonds from very strong companies. DuPont, Dow Chemical, and Ford are other companies whose bonds I think yield a tremendous amount compared to the risk that they run right now.

Now please do not run right out and buy these bonds; by the time you're reading this it will have been at least a few weeks if not a year or so from the time of this writing, and the environment could have changed. But the wonderful thing about corporate bonds is that you can sell them on any trading day at whatever is their current price—they're completely liquid. As long as I'm not holding hundreds of thousands dollars in one bond in a client's portfolios, I can sell them pretty much without a wrinkle.

Let's talk about a second income-producing security: preferred stocks, which are a little more volatile than corporate bonds as far as price movement goes. Many companies issue preferred stock as well as common stock. The difference between preferred stock and common stock is simple. The dividends on a preferred stock are "preferred" over the dividends on that same company's common stock. Let's use AT&T as an example. Right now AT&T pays about a 5% dividend on its common stock, so I can get that 5% yearly dividend, and if the stock goes up in value, I make even more money. If AT&T has a preferred stock, it cannot cut or stop the dividend on it until it completely quits paying dividends on its common stock—it's in that sense that one stock is "preferred" over the other. So it's a pretty safe bet that if a company's common stock is paying a

5.5% dividend, my preferred stock may pay a 6% or 7% dividend, a dividend that is pretty secure.

Let's think about this for a minute. We have the rest of the brokerage world, primarily a lot of independent financial advisors, and particularly those with big brokerage firms such as UBS and Merrill Lynch, using mutual funds to produce income. And yet those mutual funds, as we've already seen, have huge holding costs and all kinds of trading fees, they're very tax inefficient, and on top of that, the income they generate is much less predictable.

Compare this to preferred stock issued by a quality company such as AT&T, Wells Fargo, or JPMorgan that pays up to a 7% dividend and has complete liquidity and no hidden costs.

The only cost you're going to pay is if you're working with a financial advisor, which once again we recommend highly. You pay a management fee to that financial advisor to watch over your portfolio and to deliver a predictable return with stability of principal. So I can buy quality preferred stocks, create a 6%, 7%, maybe even a 7.5% yield, and even after paying a management fee, I get a 6% yield. Where else can I get a 6% yield with not only liquidity but also stability of principal?

So my firm likes preferred stocks. In fact, during the financial crisis I picked up Wells Fargo preferred stock for my father, and he's enjoying about an 8% to 9% yield on it. In addition to that he has also enjoyed appreciation in principal; all told he's up about 20% on his investment.

Next, let's talk about REITs—real estate investment trusts. Real estate investment trusts can also provide a very predictable income and a high degree of safety; instead of being backed by a promise to pay like a corporate bond or an equity issue like a preferred stock, a REIT is backed by real estate. (Some REITs are also backed by mortgages, which are of course indirectly backed by real estate.) Someone who has a mortgage doesn't own the real estate directly, but if he fails to pay on that mortgage, the underlying real estate can be repossessed.

A very well-known and well-managed real estate trust is paying a 12% to 14% dividend rate as I write this. Very profitable. It can fluctuate in value every day on the New York Stock Exchange, but this is a pretty attractive yield. It yields so much because Wall Street traders and investors think that there's the risk that the company is either going to cut its dividend or that some of its mortgages could default and the trust's price would go down. However, I would suggest based on the dividends that the price has gone down quite a bit already and that some of that fear has already been built into the security; we might have already experienced a bottom on that investment. It might be a wonderful opportunity to make some money on the upside as well as collecting a very nice dividend along the way.

There are two types of real estate trusts. We've been talking about real estate trusts that trade actively on an exchange, and their price fluctuates every day. If the value of the real estate goes up over time, then the value of the share price will go up as well. This can be a wonderful income-producing security for a portion of your portfolio.

The Big Three

You Pick TWO!

Safety

Liquidity

Growth

- Of course, we want all three options, but life doesn't work that way.

- Most retirees find Growth Potential and Safety of Principal to be the most important.

- That means giving up some liquidity; but that's ok because our **core** nest egg *doesn't really need it!*

If you want a higher degree of safety, then consider a *non-traded* real estate trust, which offers a simple trade-off between safety of principal and liquidity. With a non-traded real estate trust, you give up the right to sell on the open market; you typically make a time commitment of anywhere between three to seven years on the investment. What you get in exchange for that time commitment is a stable asset price of typically $10 a share. We use non-traded real estate trusts an awful lot for our clients who want steady, predictable income. The real estate in these non-traded trusts tends to be much, much newer properties, usually just purchased by the trust. So the valuation of its real estate holdings is much more current than that of the holdings embedded in other REITs that trade on exchanges. In addition to that we get a dividend that should go up over time, and after that four- to seven-year holding period, we may get appreciation of possibly as much as 20% or 30% on this real estate.

So far we've covered corporate bonds, preferred stocks, and two types of real estate investment trusts, non-traded and traded. So let's turn to a certain type of annuity. We refer to it in our practice as the *hybrid income plan.* Why would we use an annuity to generate income? One reason is that annuities were originally designed as income-generating investments. Many people use them as investment tools. They put money in them for a while and then take the money out without ever annuitizing them or using them for income, but the annuity was designed as an income vehicle.

There are a lot of bad annuities out there—you have to be very, very careful. Again, I would urge you to consult with a financial expert. But a properly designed annuity can offer some very interesting features. You can put money into a hybrid income annuity and for every year you leave the annuity alone, the value of your account grows by anywhere between 6% and 8%; that's right, 8% per year. Put $100,000 in, and the income value can be guaranteed to go to $200,000 in nine years. Now it could be better than this, but let's just say it doesn't do any better than that and we just get the guarantee. My $100,000 could grow to $200,000 in nine years, at which time I could start taking out a guaranteed income stream that I would not outlive. So on that $200,000, someone who is 70 could receive a 6% guaranteed annuity with many of these hybrid income products.

Does this mean that the investor gives up control of the principal as was the case with the old annuities? Many of you have heard, "Don't put money into an annuity; when you die, the insurance company keeps the money." That's not the way these new and improved annuities, these hybrid income plans, work. The insurance company does not keep the money. If there's any money left in the account upon your death, your heirs get it.

So let's go through this. I put in $100,000 at age 60 that is guaranteed to be at worst $200,000 when I turn 70. Now I begin to take an income stream of 6% from the annuity, $1,000 per month, $12,000 per year. That's a pretty good return from my original $100,000 investment. I can continue to take that $1,000 per month, and even if the account does not earn 8% for the first 10 years or 6% thereafter, and I live so long that the account value goes to zero because I've spent all the money, all the growth plus the original principal—if I'm still alive, the insurance company guarantees that I will continue to get my monthly checks. I can't outlive my money.

Remember earlier in the book we discussed the biggest fear for retirees, outliving their money? The problem in the old days was when we bought an annuity, we'd get a lousy 2% or 3% rate, and then again, when we'd die, the insurance company kept any money that was left over. Well, that's not how hybrid income annuities work, so they can be very, very attractive ways of producing income.

I own two annuities called indexed annuities. They have no fees, and my principal is not at any risk. In the years when the stock market goes up, I get a portion of that upside of the market—not all of it, but a portion. In return for my giving up some of the market's upside, the insurance company takes away all of the downside. If I think just about the last few years of the market, we've had basically three up years, but in between we had a horrible down year of about 40%. Well, in my first year I got about a 4% rate of return. In my second up year I got 7% rate of return. But the third year, the market was down 40%. If I would have owned the Vanguard S&P 500 Fund—and some financial tabloids say that all I need to do is buy indexed funds—I would have lost 40%. Today I still would have been way behind where I started. But with this particular indexed annuity, in the year when the market dropped 40%, I lost nothing. In fact, it's almost like I gained 40% because I beat the market by 40%. I did not gain 40%, but again, if the market drops 40%, I hold onto my principal. This is what hedge fund managers are getting paid millions and millions if not billions to do.

Now 1999, the following year, was a very interesting year, because the market increased substantially and I got a very nice rate of return on my money; I think I got 10% or 12%. That's a pretty darn good rate of return without any risk to principal. Hybrid income annuities and hybrid indexed annuities can be very, very attractive. Again, be careful—there's a lot of bad ones out there; consult with a financial expert (see chart: Fixed Index Annuities).

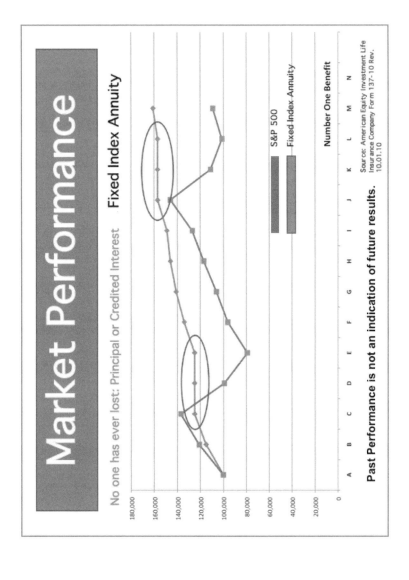

Market Performance

No one has ever lost: Principal or Credited Interest   Fixed Index Annuity

Past Performance is not an indication of future results.

S&P 500

Fixed Index Annuity

Number One Benefit

Source: American Equity Investment Life
Insurance Company Form 137-10 Rev.
10.01.10

The purpose of this chapter was to give you ideas about different income-producing securities. We have found in our practice at Johnson Brunetti that if we can deliver to clients between 5% to 8% consistent income with very, very steady principal, and in addition to that create other pieces of their portfolios that are totally safe, and then a third component that has growth potential, it's very difficult for a client to run out of money. This is why our clients feel secure in living a quality life in retirement.

THE KNOCKOUT PUNCH TO THE TAXMAN
THE ROTH IRA VERSUS TRADITIONAL RETIREMENT PLANS

Imagine being able to take a chunk of your money and remove it from the reaches of the government forever. Would you like to do that? Would that benefit you and your family?

In this chapter we will explore the differences between Roth IRAs and traditional retirement accounts such as 401(k)s, 403(b)s, 457s, and traditional IRAs. The extension of the Bush tax cuts gives us the ability to take advantage of even lower taxes on a Roth conversion, which we will talk about later. Do you think taxes are going up? Are you concerned that your children will have to pay big taxes on your retirement accounts when they inherit that money? Are you bothered by the government attacking your retirement accounts when you turn 70 1/2? Roth IRAs allow you to avoid all of these problems.

There are two ways to get money into a Roth IRA. First, if you have earned income and your adjusted gross income (AGI, the last number on the bottom front page of your 1040 form) is below the IRS limit, you can contribute $5,000 to a Roth IRA, or if 50 years old or more, you can contribute $6,000. Now the maximum AGI is less than $105,000 if you file single or $167,000 if you file married and jointly. Let me just state that again: you can contribute $5,000 to a Roth IRA if you're married and you file jointly as long as your adjusted gross income is not more than $167,000. If you're over 50, filing married, and your income is less than $167,000, then you can contribute $6,000. The limits noted are for 2010, but they do not change more than about 10% at the most per year. You can decide how applicable this is to you and simply get the current numbers online.

The second way that you can get money into a Roth is through a conversion from a traditional retirement account such as a 401(k), a 403(b), or an IRA. The catch here is that the amount I convert from a traditional retirement account to a Roth needs to be added to my income, so income taxes will be owed. For example, if I convert $200,000 from a traditional IRA to a Roth IRA, I will add the $200,000 to my income in the year that I convert. That's the bad news.

The good news is that that $200,000 I converted will grow tax free as long as I leave it in the Roth. If I leave it alone for 20 years, at a 7.2% average annual return over that period, my $200,000 will be worth $800,000, and I can now spend the $800,000 tax-free.

The following charts and explanations illustrate four ways to handle a Roth conversion and the tax cost of each. If you think taxes are going up and you want to keep the government out of your future retirement savings, and if you're able to leave that money alone for a while, it probably would benefit you to convert to a Roth IRA.

SO THESE ARE THE FOUR DIFFERENT WAYS TO CONVERT TO A ROTH.

• You can pay taxes from the current IRA while you convert it.

• You can pay taxes from outside the IRA that's being converted.

• You can pay no taxes by using nonretirement money to invest in a special tax-advantaged investment program, thus offsetting the taxes.

• You can pay the tax from life insurance proceeds, in a sense using someone else's money to pay the taxes.

On the following charts I will illustrate the differences between the four different strategies.

JohnsonBRUNETTI
CONNECTICUT'S RETIREMENT & INVESTMENT SPECIALISTS

4 ways to convert to a Roth

1. Pay taxes from the current IRA

2. Pay taxes from outside the current IRA

3. Pay no taxes by using non-IRA money to invest in special tax-advantaged investment programs

4. Pay tax from Life insurance proceeds

Strategy number one involves paying taxes from the current IRA. In our example here, Joe Torre, former manager of the New York Yankees and now manager of the Los Angeles Dodgers, takes $200,000 out of his IRA and converts $150,000 of it to a Roth. He sets aside the other $50,000 to pay the taxes. As we can see on our chart, the $150,000 at 7% grows over 10 years to $295,000, and over 20 years to $580,000, while the government gets $50,000 in taxes. The good news is that Mr. Torre, if he's alive 20 years from now, can use that $580,000 and spend it in one lump sum if he wanted to completely tax-free. If he passes away, the $580,000 is inherited by his beneficiaries, and they can spend the money completely tax-free or leave it in a Roth IRA to continue to grow for their beneficiaries. Those beneficiaries have to take out a little bit each year, but it's not much; the majority of the money can grow tax-free.

JohnsonBRUNETTI
CONNECTICUT'S RETIREMENT & INVESTMENT SPECIALISTS

Strategy #1 – Pay Taxes from the current IRA

Joe Torre takes $200,000 out of his IRA and converts $150,000 of it to a ROTH.

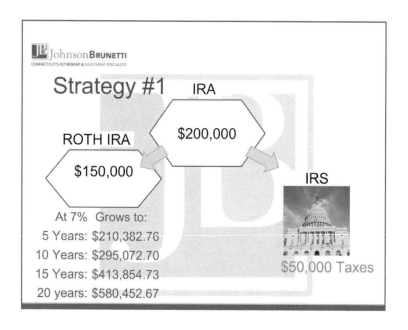

Strategy number two calls for paying taxes from outside the current IRA. This gives us the ability to convert the entire $200,000 IRA. So in this example, Red Sox former manager Terry Francona takes $200,000 out of his IRA and converts it all to a Roth, using other funds to pay the $50,000 in taxes. That $200,000, at 7%, grows in 20 years to $773,000. There's a big difference by leaving that $50,000 inside the Roth IRA and paying IRS taxes from another source. The chart that compares strategy number one to strategy number two demonstrates that the difference by paying the taxes from outside funds is almost $100,000 after 10 years and is almost $200,000 after 20 years. That's the power of dollars compounding tax-free inside the Roth IRA.

The lesson here on strategy number one versus strategy number two: it always makes sense to pay the taxes from outside the IRA being converted if possible.

Strategy #2 – Pay Taxes from Outside the current IRA

Terry Francona takes $200,000 out of his IRA and converts it all to a ROTH and uses funds from another account to pay the $50,000 in taxes.

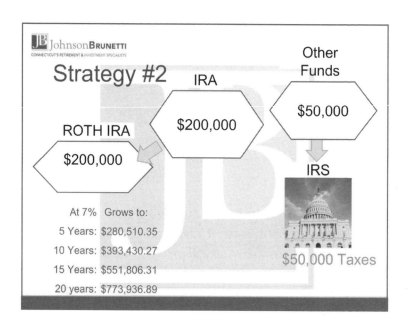

Strategy #1 Vs. Strategy #2

At 7%, grows to:	Strategy #1 Taxes Paid from INSIDE	Strategy #2 Taxes Paid from OUTSIDE
5 years	$210,382.76	$280,510.35
10 years	$295,072.70	$393,430.27
15 years	$413,854.73	$551,806.31
20 years	$580,452.67	$773,936.89

Now strategy number three is conversion to Roth but zeroing out the taxes. In this example let's use George Steinbrenner, an interesting fellow who owned the Yankees of course for many years, and his family still controls the ball club. He hated taxes so much that he decided to die in 2010, the one year we had no inheritance taxes. Mr. Steinbrenner's net worth was estimated to be $1.6 billion. If he had died in 2011, his money would have been taxed at a much higher rate, and if he had died in 2009, his money would have been taxed at a very, very high rate. But as he died in 2010, his $1.6 billion passed tax-free to his heirs, while had he died in 2011, his estate taxes would have been approximately $550 million—a huge difference.

In this example, Mr. Steinbrenner takes $200,000 out of his IRA and converts it to a Roth IRA. He uses funds from another account to invest in a tax-advantaged oil and natural gas program, which allows a deduction that zeroes out the taxes. It also creates for him a very attractive income stream.

So let's go over this example on the chart that illustrates strategy number three. Mr. Steinbrenner's entire $200,000, at 7% interest, grows to $773,936.89, as is the case with strategy number two. But he also takes $230,000 from another account and puts it into an oil and gas program, which allows for a deduction of about 85% of what he contributed. So he puts $200,000 of income on his tax return because of the Roth IRA conversion but subtracts $200,000 of income because of the deduction for investing in the oil and gas program—thus completely zeroing out the taxes.

Another benefit of the oil and gas program is that it creates monthly income after about a year that could last as long as 25 years; and if the price of energy goes up, he's a direct participant in the value of energy crisis, because his monthly income checks go up proportionately.

A word of caution here: investigate thoroughly any oil and gas program, as they are not for everybody; you need to be an accredited investor to get involved in all the programs I know about. The definition of accredited investor is someone with a net worth of $1 million.

A second word of caution—really a word of *warning*—is that there are good operators and bad operators in the oil and gas business. Consult with a financial professional who has been investing in these programs for clients for quite some time so that you can get expertise on which programs are good and which programs are bad.

JohnsonBRUNETTI
CONNECTICUT'S RETIREMENT & INVESTMENT SPECIALISTS

Strategy #3 – Conversion to ROTH & Zero Out Taxes

George Steinbrenner takes $200,000 out of his IRA and converts it all to a ROTH and uses funds from another account to invest in a tax-advantaged oil & natural gas program to zero out the taxes and create a long-term income stream.

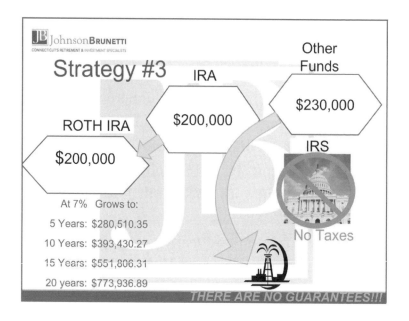

Strategy number four is a little different. In this case, instead of doing a Roth conversion today, we're going to defer that Roth conversion. In this example we use Ty Cobb and Mrs. Cobb. Ty is a real stickler; he doesn't want to pay any taxes or even change his tax return before he has to. So Ty tells Mrs. Cobb that he is going to buy a life insurance policy so that when he dies, she will have cash to convert his entire IRA, because life insurance cash is tax-free. Strategy number four, then, shows that the $200,000 IRA grows at 6% to $641,000 when Ty Cobb dies at 85. Notice that we have a growth rate of 6% here, because he's going to extract 1% per year from the IRA to pay for the life insurance policy that will go tax-free to Mrs. Cobb when he dies. These proceeds are more than enough to pay the taxes and convert the entire $641,000 to a Roth IRA, and she has her $641,000 tax-free forever to use as she needs it or to pass on to her children.

Strategy #4 – Use Life Insurance Company's Money to Pay the Taxes at Death

Mrs. Cobb uses life insurance to pay the taxes to convert Ty Cobb's IRA to a Roth at the time of his death.

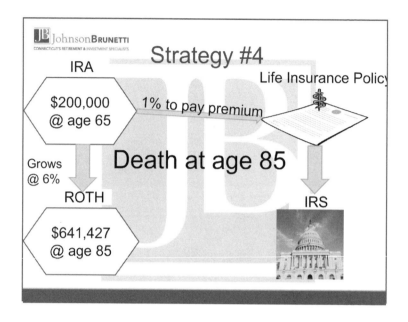

The key point with these four strategies on converting to a Roth IRA is that if you think taxes are going up and you want to take control of your taxes by locking in current rates, a Roth conversion is probably something to seriously consider. Once again, consult a financial professional, because there are many different moving parts to this Roth IRA conversion, and you want to make sure you have examined all the options and have chosen the correct one for you.

HOW TO CHOOSE THE RIGHT FINANCIAL ADVISOR

In this chapter I will list nine important matters you should keep in mind when you try to find the correct financial advisor to work with. It is important that there is "chemistry" between you, that there is a good fit and a sharing of values. There also should be a feeling that the person understands you. We'll go over these elements in this chapter.

JohnsonBRUNETTI
CONNECTICUT'S RETIREMENT & INVESTMENT SPECIALISTS

We are Independent

- Different from...

Merrill Lynch   Smith Barney   Amerprise
AG Edwards   Wachovia   Wells Fargo
Morgan Stanley   Citigroup   Advest
RBC   Bank of America
JP Morgan Chase   Barclays

JohnsonBRUNETTI
CONNECTICUT'S RETIREMENT & INVESTMENT SPECIALISTS

Independent?
What does that mean?

Is it important?

You decide

1. INDEPENDENT

It is very important that the financial advisor you choose be independent, someone who is not an employee of a large firm. There are many firms at which brokers and advisors can work. I started in the business 26 years ago as an employee of a big brokerage firm, and we employees were told what products and funds to recommend. We were told that what we had to sell was perfect for everyone. When our sales manager had certain stocks that he would decide we should push in a certain month, guess what? Those stocks were what most people ended up owning.

I soon came to realize that this was the wrong approach, but unfortunately it still goes on today. Let's take for example a very large Wall Street brokerage firm. First of all, if you work for such a firm, the people you work with are employees of that firm, so their primary responsibility is to that firm, not to you. Their job is to increase shareholder value for that particular firm. You're just a customer.

But if you work with an independent financial advisor, then you are the only person to whom that advisor answers. An ethical independent financial advisor does not have an agenda or a list of stocks to push.

It is very important that you find an independent financial advisor.

2. CHEMISTRY

The second important consideration is "chemistry." It's very important that you feel the person you're talking to understands you. If you are a husband and wife, make sure the person talks to both of you and also listens to both of you. If for one moment you feel that a broker is dismissing you or your feelings or is insulting or is coming across as arrogant, this is the wrong person to work with. You need to choose an advisor who understands you, who listens to you, and who will put together a financial plan that fits your needs and goals.

3. EMPATHY

Empathy. Does the advisor understand you and feel like you do when it comes to your important issues? You may have a special-needs child who requires special planning. You may come from a very poor family, one that lived through the depression, and you're worried about running out of money. Can that advisor relate? It's critical that the advisor listen and feel empathy for your particular fears. Another clue here that you're working with the wrong advisor is he or she does not understand or does not listen.

4. ADEQUATE STAFFING

Staffing is a critical issue: it's where the rubber meets the road in today's financial world. Make sure the advisor you work with has plenty of service staff, and do so by simply asking. I know some firms where a broker handles hundreds of accounts without a full-time assistant, maybe sharing one with another broker. This isn't going to work very well. Two things can happen. Number one, the service level drops; number two, the broker or advisor has to constantly answer every phone call, every service inquiry. If I am talking to my advisor, I want one who is thinking about my investments, one who deals one-on-one with clients, not one bogged down by service inquiries and other issues that could be handled by a service assistant or a customer service representative.

Our firm has six advisors and a team of 9 full-time and 3 part-time people. Each advisor has four backup people, and that's a pretty good ratio. I think you want at least a two-to-one ratio, two assistants per advisor in the firm. So a firm with two advisors should have at least four staff people backing them up. If you get lower than this in today's economy, when investment firms and insurance companies push more and more paperwork out to the financial firm that they used to do for their advisors, it is going to be very hard for that broker to handle your account.

5. COMMUNITY RECOGNITION

The broker or advisor you choose should have a recognized name in the community. Let's think about a company like Disney. In Orlando, if somebody even writes the word *Disney* on a sign, Disney comes after them to take that word down. Disney makes sure that if it has the legal right to force the issue, it will do it simply because it wants to protect its reputation, a reputation second to none.

Other companies such as McDonalds and Coca Cola that have a very high level of service and brand recognition will do almost anything to protect that brand. They will decide not to take certain customers because they worry that those customers might be the complaining type, and the companies want to protect their reputation and their brand.

The same goes for financial advisors. Financial advisors who have a recognized name in a community will be very careful to bend over backward to do the right thing because they have spent years building their strong reputations and don't want to do anything to tarnish them. Choose an advisor who has a well-recognized name in the community.

6. AUTHOR = AUTHORITY

It is important that your advisor be an author. Has yours written articles? Has yours authored books? Does he have any kind of ownership of publications out there, including a website? Is the website part of a big firm like Merrill Lynch or Ameriprise, or is it independent?

Independent advisors will tend to have their own websites, not websites that are linked to big brokerage houses. It's helpful to know that your advisor has the expertise and the independence to write about subjects that are relevant to you.

7. MEDIA PRESENCE

This goes along with number six—find an advisor who has a media presence, someone the media trusts for knowledge and advice. TV and radio stations typically have certain people they go to in the community who are able to speak on a number of different subjects. Has your advisor been on TV or the radio in the role of a local expert? This can be a good indication of a good reputation.

8. A GOOD BUSINESS PERSON

Does your advisor know how to run a business? This goes back to the difference between an independent advisor and one who is just an employee of the firm. How somebody can handle millions of dollars of other people's money and have no clue as to how to run a business is beyond me. It's also beyond me that somebody would choose to work with an advisor who has no employees, who has no banking relationship or even a business checkbook, and who does not spend his or her own money on marketing and reputation. This is inconceivable to me.

Find an advisor who is independent and also understands the ins and outs of running a business, including hiring and firing employees, supervising customer service staff, and delegating issues as they come up instead of doing absolutely everything themselves.

9. GIVING BACK

Last but not least, find an advisor who gives back to his or her community, one willing to put money back into the community and not just for the sake of publicity, such as sponsoring charity auctions so that an advisor can be seen with a bunch of rich people, not that there is anything wrong with that. I'm talking about someone who is honestly trying to give back to the community and to help when it comes to helping those in need.

Keep these nine considerations in mind when you are in the process of choosing a financial advisor. Try also to make your own list of your own values, as some on my list might not be important to you. But start with my list of nine and begin to narrow down the advisors in your community; it is very possible that in an area like Connecticut, my state that has thousands of licensed investment advisors, you may come up with only 20 to choose from. But then you can begin to interview them, talking and listening, and end up with the one who is the best fit for you.

10. CREDENTIALS

Your advisor or people on their team should have certain credentials. The CERTIFIED FINANCIAL PLANNER™ or CFP® is the most highly regarded in the financial advice world. CFP® professionals must complete extensive training and experience and are held to high ethical standards. The CFP is awarded by The College for Financial Planning.

Other designations that are highly esteemed are ChFC® and CFA. The ChFC® is awarded by The

American College and is usually awarded to people that have a life insurance agency background. It is a well respected credential that takes quite a bit of study to complete.

The CFA or Chartered Financial Analyst is very difficult to receive. It deals mostly with the analysis of securities, balance sheets, profit & loss statements and things that would be used by people managing money, but not giving advice to individuals like we do. Most Mutual Fund Managers are CFA's. If you are looking for one on one financial advice you would probably not seek out a CFA, but your advisor or their team should have a CFP® available at the firm.

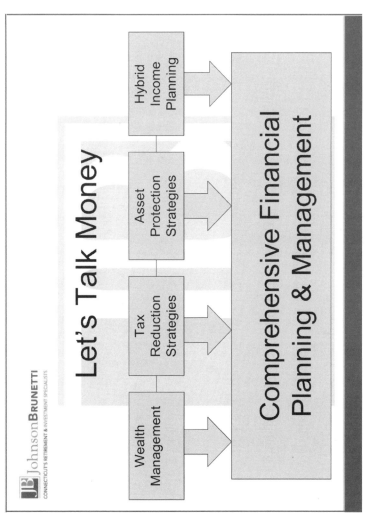

The Four Areas of Service We Provide for our Clients

WA